DRESSAGE
EXPLAINED

DRESSAGE
EXPLAINED

CAROL GREEN

WARD LOCK

Acknowledgements

There are several people to whom I must express a debt of
gratitude and acknowledgement of invaluable assistance, both in my
career and in the preparation of this book. First, to Mrs Hatton-Hall,
for all her kindness, help and encouragement throughout the years
of my own training. To Marie Stokes, for her great assistance and
technical advice, and for so ably appearing in the photographs, taken
at her Walton Heath Livery Yard in Tadworth, Surrey. To Lt-Col
W. J. W. Froud, National Instructor, The British Horse Society. To
Sue Hatherley, a National Champion, for her encouragement and
help. To Peter Phillips whose photographs have captured the essence
of dressage. Thanks also to Kit Houghton for the photographs on
pages 9, 13, 29 and 52; and to Bob Langrish for that on page 80. An
acknowledgement also to the British Horse Society, whose dressage rules
and official procedure for dressage competitions I have used as a source of
reference.
Finally, my thanks and good wishes to all who read this book for
their contribution towards making dressage better understood,
better performed and better enjoyed by everyone.

© Carol Green 1974, 1977, 1989

This edition published in Great Britain in 1989
by Ward Lock Limited, Artillery House,
Artillery Row, London SW1P 1RT, a Cassell Company

Reprinted 1990

Previously published as
'A Horseman's Handbook'

Printed in Spain by Graficas Reunidas

Cover photography by Kit Houghton

British Library Cataloguing in Publication Data

Green, Carol
    Dressage explained. – (*Ward Lock's Riding School*)
    1. Dressage
    I. Title   II. Series
    798.2'3   SF309.5

    ISBN 0-7063-6780-4

Contents

Preface

In the following pages I have tried to explain from my own experience the full meaning of dressage. I am essentially a practical person, and I hope that my thoughts will show you that much enjoyment can be gained by schooling and improving your horse's way of going. If his paces are light, regular, harmonious and obedient not only will he be a pleasure to ride but his performance both over fences and on the flat will naturally be better.

Dressage means the training of the horse in deportment, response, balance, and athletic ability whereby he is able to submit generously to the control of his rider. The horse should be calm and supple, being 'one' with his rider, his work should show freedom and regularity to his paces. In all his movements lightness, harmony and the engagement of the hindquarters should be apparent. The horse thus gives the impression of moving and carrying himself of his own accord, being confident and attentive, moving forward absolutely straight between the rider's hand and leg. Dressage is interesting and absorbing, requiring hard daily work both in the school and out hacking. It is normally a means to an end in that it is a series of gymnastic exercises to improve the balance, suppleness, and agility of the horse, thus enabling him to jump, race, or play polo with the minimum amount of strain on his limbs. However, dressage tests are now a separate competition of their own at many shows; consequently dressage is beginning to have a place as a sport and hold its own among other show events.

Foreword

It is absolutely necessary that all keen riders learn, at an early stage, the meaning and the importance of the word 'dressage'. All too often beginners are allowed to start jumping before they have learnt the basic aids of elementary riding, and the sooner they realise that dressage, in its simpler form, is not difficult or boring, and should be tackled enthusiastically from the start, the sooner they will rise to the dizzy heights of success — for it is not just dressage competitions that require obedience, balance, lightness and sensitivity of aids. Hunting, hacking, showjumping and eventing, to mention just a few of the many spheres of equestrianism, will all benefit enormously from a basic knowledge and ability for dressage.

Carol Green has written this book for all age groups and has admirably contributed to the ever increasing population of horse lovers in portraying, in the simplest form, the progressive stages of training a horse with the maximum of interest and minimum of difficulty, and I hope that this book will encourage all riding enthusiasts to take a greater interest in the art of dressage and its meaning.

Sue Halterly

1 The seat of the rider

The rider must learn through practice, training and technique to
develop a correct seat and thus ride by balance and feel, using
only the most subtle aids. The first aim of the dressage rider is to
achieve this correct seat and the most positive way of accomplishing
it is to work on the lunge rein. The rider can then concentrate on
keeping in balance with and following the movement of the horse,
sitting in the proper attitude. A trainer with a good eye will place
the rider in a proper posture to give him a good feeling; being
very quick to correct, immediately the rider loses this position.
If, as is my intention, I am to give the fullest assistance to the
intending exponent of dressage, it will help enormously if from
this point I adopt the friendly rapport that one enjoys at every
riding school and stables. I shall, therefore, try to avoid impersonal
expressions like 'the rider' and instead address myself face to face
with you, the reader, the one who by dint of hard work and
boundless patience aims to master the skilled and enjoyable art of

Left: Rehearsing a half pass for a dressage test

Below: Competing in a pony club dressage event

dressage. First, you must sit in the centre and the lowest part of the saddle, in an erect position, your weight evenly distributed over three points, which are the two pelvic bones and the crotch. A straight line should be envisaged through the ears, shoulders, hip and heels, the shoulders being above the hips in all movements. The feet should rest naturally in the stirrups with the heels below the level of the toe. The lower part of your leg should hang loosely by the weight of the leg alone to the barrel of the horse, the inside part of the leg in a position to be applied calmly and quietly as a delicate but effective aid. Relaxation is most important, the aim being to achieve an upright straight posture, with complete relaxation of all muscles. The upper arm should form almost a right-angle to the forearm, the arm being held loosely to the side, the fingers closed around the rein, the hands held approximately four inches from the body. The best way to achieve a good seat in harmony and balance with the horse is by progressive work on the lunge line.

Lungeing is an excellent exercise enabling the development of greater feel, suppleness, balance, and depth of seat more quickly and thoroughly than any other method I have experienced. Indeed, the Spanish Riding School in Vienna value its merits so highly that all pupils receiving instruction at the Spanish School are put on the lunge line for part of their training, be they young novice riders, or the most experienced. On the lunge line the rider can concentrate on developing a good, secure, supple, well-balanced and independent seat without having to think about controlling the horse. The trainer has the opportunity to analyse his pupil and correct faults of straightness and correctness of seat as soon as they occur. If the rider is worked to suitable music it helps to develop a sense of feel and rhythm which is a fundamental in the art of riding. Lungeing is, however, very strenuous and may cause fatigue, soreness and stiffness; the trainer should guard against this at all costs, as quite obviously if the pupil is tired the muscles will become tense and tight, thus making it impossible to relax and co-ordinate the limbs correctly in a good attitude. So my advice to you is, begin with short lunge lessons of only 20 minutes' duration initially, progressing to 45 minutes as you become fitter, deeper and better balanced. It is a mistake to work for too long a period without stirrups as this again will lead to pulled muscles and tension.

2 The paces of the horse

I have already mentioned that in dressage one is striving to develop
the basic paces of the horse when ridden, so that they are light,
regular and harmonious. In order to be able to do this one must
first examine the horse's ordinary paces — discussed in the next
few paragraphs.

The halt The horse should stand motionless with his weight evenly
distributed over all four legs, being straight through his spine.
The horse should be attentive and alert, the head a little in front
of the vertical with the neck raised and the horse flexed from the
poll. You should be able to maintain a light contact with the
horse's mouth and the horse should be naturally ready to spring
forward at the slightest indication from the trainer. Any transition
either upwards or downwards should be smooth, active, and
accurately ridden, the horse being obedient to your aid.

Halt   Notice the alert attitude of this halt. A good entry to any
dressage test

Above. Here one sees the rider with a light rein contact allowing the horse to walk with energetic strides

Right: A dressage competition for pony owners with an unusual variation

The walk This is a pace of four-time, in which the legs move separately in a marching pace one after another in a sequence of near-fore, off-hind, off-fore, and lastly the near-hind. You must sit still with a light rein contact allowing the horse to walk with energetic strides. There are four steps to one stride at the pace walk. It is, however, one of the most difficult paces at which to ride, because in walk the imperfections in training are the most marked, showing very often that the degree of collection is not in accordance with the stage of schooling of the horse but is in fact hurried and forced.

There are four recognised walks: medium, collected, extended and free. In the *Medium Walk* the horse should be free and full of energy while completely straight, being always obedient and responsive to the rider's aids. The hindlegs must be active and diligent and not dragging behind. The horse must maintain the

The medium trot, the collected trot and the extended trot

Above. The rider rises allowing the impulsion of the horse to propel him forward from behind

Above right. Here the rider remains in the saddle being close to the horse. Notice the symmetrical and rhythmic steps of this horse

Below right. Notice here how the horse moves with longer strides

correct sequence with no head tossing which might be a sign of an insufficient use of the hindquarters, or too much use of the rider's hand. At the *Collected Walk* the horse's body is completely straight, and he is accepting the bit with a constant but gentle contact. The pace should remain marching and energetic, with well defined and elevated steps, the hindlegs springing elastically from the ground. In the collected walk the horse will be in a compressed form moving with a slightly shorter stride than at the ordinary walk, the hindfeet touching the ground behind the footprints of the forefeet. The *Extended Walk*, however, is the pace at which the horse should cover as much ground as possible, calmly and quietly so as not to lose the regularity of his steps. With this longer stride the hindfeet touch the ground in front of the footprints of the forefeet. The horse, although accepting the bridle,

14

The medium canter

The horse moving calmly forward with the near foreleg leading

should take a little more contact than at the ordinary walk. The impulsion and activity is maintained with the horse walking with a determined and positive stride, the forehead being a little in front of the vertical. The *Free Walk* is that in which the horse stretches down with its head and neck, looking for the contact with the bit, relaxing its top line and moving with long easy strides. The hind feet overlap the tracks of the fore feet, the neck is long and the horse's head is in front of the vertical.

The trot This is a pace of two-time, the legs moving in diagonal pairs. The 'right diagonal' is the near-hind and the off-fore, and the 'left diagonal' the off-hind and the near-fore. The horse should move with calm equal strides forward and straight. At the *Medium Trot* the horse is not 'collected' but works with good energetic strides, the impulsion coming from the hindquarters, causing him to have a slightly long neck with his head a little in front of the vertical. The *Working Trot* — "this is a pace between the medium and the collected trot in which a horse, not yet ready or trained for collected movements, shows itself properly balanced and with a supple poll remaining on the bit, goes forward with even, elastic steps and good hock action" – quoted from F.E.I. definitions of Paces and Movements article 404.4.

In the *Collected Trot* the horse will work with more elevated steps showing plenty of forward impulsion and gaiety in his steps. The steps must be symmetrical and rhythmic thus showing lightness and greater mobility of each stride. In the *Extended Trot* the horse covers as much ground as possible. He lengthens his stride, remaining on the bit with a light contact. The horse's neck becomes longer, the forehead being slightly in front of the vertical with equal but elastic reins. The horse must be completely straight, maintaining rhythm and cadence; the front legs must step and touch the ground at the spot at which they are pointing. In the extended trot the rider must be careful not to demand too much too soon thus unbalancing the horse, being sure at all times that the driving action of the hindquarters is in the right proportion to the general forward impulsion and stage of training.

The canter **The canter is a pace of three-time; by this I mean that there are three definite steps to make one stride of canter, for instance the sequence is as follows: left hindleg, left diagonal, right foreleg followed by a period of suspension with all four legs in the air**

The collected
canter The outline of the horse is one of roundness, the horse showing obvious impulsion, being in his shortened form

before taking the next stride. There are three recognised canter paces, the medium, collected and the extended.

In the *Medium Canter* the horse should be working calmly forward and straight with the inner front foot in front of the inner hind-foot. The three-time sequence should be well marked, and the horse seen to be swinging in his back with the rider sitting still in the saddle gently absorbing the movement of this comfortable pace. The *Working Canter* — "this is a pace between the medium and the collected canter in which a horse, not yet ready or trained for collected movements, shows itself properly balanced and with a supple poll remaining on the bit, goes forward with even, light and cadenced strides and good hock action" — quoted from F.E.I. definitions of Paces and Movements article 405.2.

With the *Collected Canter* a clear three-time beat must be maintained at all times with the hindlegs placed as far under as possible. The head and neck will be raised, the action of the hindlegs allowing the horse to spring forward with a more elevated stride. The *Extended Canter* is a difficult pace to develop and must be done by gently applying the forward pushing aids and not allowing the horse to go forward in jerks. The observer standing on the ground should receive the impression that the strides do not grow more hurried and faster but that they grow longer and gain more ground. The horse's neck becomes longer, the forehead being slightly in front of the vertical, the rhythm and cadence being well maintained.

A *transition* is the term given to a change from any of the above paces, going from one to another. With the novice horse each of the transitions should be progressive, moving from halt, walk, trot through to canter, or from canter progressively through to walk and halt. All transitions should be carried through gently but distinctly and with plenty of impulsion. In a dressage test a rough or abrupt transition will be marked as a fault; naturally, therefore, the horse's stage of training must be such that his transitions are smooth, unhurried and forward going, and they must also be accurate. The horse must learn to respond to the rider's aid at the slightest indication so that a transition is carried out at the exact place indicated. The paces explained are the working paces which will be required of you in your early dressage tests. In novice tests or Pony Club tests you will not be asked for any collected paces, but only to ride your horse through the working paces. The judge will be looking to see if your horse is free and forward going, obedient and responsive to your aids and with his impulsion coming from the hindquarters; he will also note the horse's way of going, his stage of training and whether or not he is ready to compete at this level.

18

3. Figures, turns, circles, serpentines, school movements

In order that you may increase the suppleness, athletic ability and obedience of your horse it is necessary for you to be aware of the various school movements, loops, and serpentines which are ridden at all paces, and practise them. These movements will improve the suppleness of your horse and also make him more responsive and obedient to your leg aids.

The usual turns and figures ridden in a school or manège are on a single track, changing the rein by turning down the centre and going to the opposite track, riding loops, circles, voltes, turn on the forehand, *demi-pirouettes*, serpentines and changes of direction within the circle. All these movements should first be practised at the walk, as at this pace you and your horse will find it easier to perform them. As the horse's balance improves then you should progress through to trot and ride the movements at the faster paces. The turn on the forehand, however, should be performed at the halt, and the *demi-pirouette* at the walk, with walk well marked and energetic, showing plenty of impulsion. The horse should be bent in the direction of the movement, so by working your horse with plenty of changes of direction it should be possible for you to make him more obedient and responsive to your aids. Very often the horse tends to lose impulsion on the turns and this must be anticipated: ride him energetically and firmly forward so as not to lose the rhythm of the stride, thus maintaining the impulsion coming from behind and avoiding the horse shortening his steps on the turn.

By working your horse on turns, circles and transitions you will begin to improve his suppleness and athletic ability, and also his balance. The balance of the horse is very important. Before the horse begins his training he has natural balance, but once he gets a rider on his back he loses this and has to maintain his balance with a rider; this, of course, he finds much more difficult. As a young horse in his natural state, two-thirds of his weight is on the front legs when grazing. The trainer tries to encourage the horse to shift his point of balance back, so that the weight is equally distributed. I am sure you will have noticed that when a young horse is apprehensive he prepares to move at speed by raising his head and neck; his weight is then shifted back with his hindlegs coming well under him in a collected position. When the horse extends, however, his head is well out and forward; he is not able to extend his toe beyond his nose, and this is why many racehorse owners use a sheepskin noseband to encourage the extension of the horse's head and neck. From the normal balanced state one must go on to

*The turn on
the forehand* Here the horse is asked to move away from the rider's leg, the acting
hand and leg being used on the same side

develop what is called fluid balance; this is the shifting of the
horse's point of balance smoothly forward and back without
jolting the horse and rider. The horse is, therefore, more comfortable and does not overtax any one part of his body. From this
fluid balance one must then strive for rhythm and cadence. Both
of these are very important, cadence being perfect rhythm with
added impulsion, thus producing a moment of suspension, for
example when trotting over cavalletti or a stallion turning out
into a field of mares. Rhythm is the regular, well defined step of
the horse at all paces, maintaining uniformity of stride.
If you are starting from the beginning with your young horse
and hope to train him for dressage don't break him in when too
young — ponies possibly at two years old, as they develop far more
quickly than horses, but it is best to wait until three years old.
Begin with gentle lungeing to develop balance, strengthen
muscles and teach a little discipline; all of this will do no harm

provided you are careful to work on very large circles of about 24 metres. Personally I think it is best to break at three years, just get the horse going, slipping along through the lanes in the country with an older horse, easily enjoying his walk. Then turn him out for six months and leave him to grow and keep developing on the right lines for another year. Bring him up at four years and start again from the beginning. The lessons of the previous spring will be remembered and he will go much better. It is instinctive for him to work happily for man as most horses are naturally docile. The natural centre of gravity of a horse lies at the spot where a line drawn from the point of the shoulder to the point of the buttock crosses another running from the withers to the ground. The nearer to that point the rider is positioned, the easier on the horse, hence my earlier stress on the importance of the seat.

The trainer must try to understand the mentality of every horse. To develop balance, five important facts must be considered. Take into account the conformation and temperament of the animal, the level of the ground on which he is working, the natural speed at which the horse works, the nature of the ground – heavy going, hard roads, iron hard ground, heavy sand in a school. Consider also the weight of the rider. For example, a well proportioned, well bred youngster carrying a lightweight over springy level turf will find his point of balance and go along comfortably. If, however, the horse is badly proportioned, the rider heavy and the going rough, the horse will find it difficult to rebalance himself. This is why heavy plain cobs and heavyweight hunters should be broken in later than ponies and better bred horses, and then the training must be slow. They develop late and find it difficult to rebalance with their rider's weight on top. The trainer must give the horse a progressive course of balancing and developing exercises, remembering that the average horse is not fully developed until six years old.

A good way to develop balance is by a progressive course on the lunge, with a saddle on; making a circle, using wide turns until the horse can easily move away without losing rhythm or impulsion. From the lunge work go on and begin transitions by increase and decrease of pace, both on a loose rein and on a contact. It is a good idea to work on a loose rein so that the horse does not always depend on the rider's hand. Practise transitions to halt, rein back, and then ride forward, going progressively through the transitions to trot and canter.

Although we are chiefly concerned with dressage, I believe that all types of suppling exercises are good for training and balance, and would suggest that at this stage you begin working over trotting

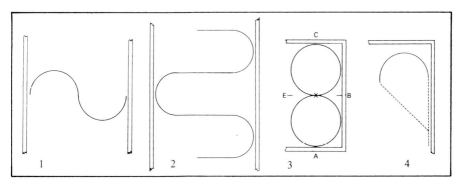

Some simple school movements

1. Half circle right 10 metres. Half circle left
2. A serpentine three loops, each loop going to the side of the arena
3. A 20 metre circle going from track to track
4. A *demi-volte*

poles and then jumping grids and combination fences. This work teaches the horse the quick shift of balance from front to rear, developing fluidity of balance and suppleness. It is an athletic exercise which develops the muscles of the back, loins and gaskin. It will encourage the horse to leap from his hocks by correct placement into a fence thus improving his balance on landing. Combination fences give a horse a sense of stride into a fence teaching him to work confidently and calmly.

In the horse schooled for dressage we are looking for good free forward movement with the horse working calmly, obediently and actively. It is important therefore that he understands the aids and responds to the leg effortlessly at the slightest indication from the rider. By systematic and regular work it is possible to develop the horse's natural paces so that he will perform when asked, showing the lightness and presence with which nature has endowed him. With this training it is vital that the horse is not allowed to become bored or stale; he must have variety in his work which will allow him to sparkle. His training programme should include work both in the school and outside, plenty of hill work, using loops and serpentines to develop the top line of the horse. Lunge him two or three times a week using changes of tempo to make him more supple in his back and develop fluid balance. Lastly, if you are in a suitable area, remember that riding must be fun. It will do no harm – and probably do both of you a lot of good – to hack quietly across country admiring the scenery and enjoying the luxury of being alone and one with the horse. It has often been said that there is no secret so close as that between master and horse.

4 Impulsion and collection

I would like to talk at some length about collection and impulsion, both of which are very important in the training of your horse. We have already discussed the importance of balance as it applies to the young horse and I must here stress that the horse must be balanced before any collection is achieved. It is possible to have impulsion without collection, but impossible to have collection without impulsion. It is vital therefore that the horse goes **forward,** as without this forward movement, collection will not be realised. In the course of training your young horse it will help you to ride as many different horses as can be made available to you, also to watch good and bad horses working. In this way you can learn to see collection and also to feel it.

By watching good riders and well trained horses work I hope that you will begin to understand the importance of achieving impulsion and collection and what in fact you are working to achieve. The well educated rider will produce collection tactfully and firmly, by first establishing that the horse is going forward. How often one sees the horse reduce his pace and lose impulsion going through a corner or turn. It is natural for the horse to lose energy on changes of direction and the rider must anticipate this so that more energy can be created in order that he maintains the same rhythm through all changes of direction and turns. If your horse does not go forward he will never be able to achieve collection. This is why the rider must train the horse to respond immediately to the lightest aid, moving lightly and energetically forward.

I think you may have seen horses working, and sometimes competing, with most of their weight on their forehand. This means that the horse is unbalanced and no matter how smooth the transitions appear to be, the horse will lose marks in a competition because it shows a fundamental fault in training. These horses with so much weight on their shoulders are basically wrong and will not progress to more advanced work unless they are first taken back to the beginning and their training restarted. With the more experienced dressage judges you will find that the horse that moves with good active paces and impulsion, going forward and straight, should get better marks than the horse that is going on its forehand, with glaring faults in training, although these imperfections may be disguised by the accuracy of the test. Naturally, however, one must strive to have the horse going correctly and accurately.

The basic paces of the horse are important, and one should look at these carefully when considering the overall picture of the young dressage horse in one's mind. His mouth should be closed with a relaxed jaw; if the horse resists in his mouth and sets his jaw, the bit will be held crookedly and therefore it will be impossible for the rider to achieve true collection. The trot should be regular and rhythmical with the horse lengthening and shortening his stride when asked. Sometimes, one finds horses that seem to 'chew the bit' making their mouths very wet. This is *not* correct, contrary to what many people think. The bit should be held lightly in the mouth with the mouth closed, the weight of both reins being absolutely even. If the rider imagines one ounce of weight in each rein the contact will be good. The rider should not have two pounds in the left hand and nothing in the right! In a competition the rider will lose marks if the mouth of the horse is open. Very often when this happens the tongue has been drawn back or even put over the bit and this quite obviously is a bad habit which again shows incorrect training. With the well trained horse the mouth will be wet, but it does not become wet by the horse

Tara, an honest useful type of pony, who is well suited to Pony Club dressage tests, and events

'chewing his bit', as many people believe, but by the action of the gland which produces the moisture stimulated by the movement of the gullet. Horses that you may have seen with very wet mouths are probably playing with the bit, fighting it or lying very heavy on the rider's hand. These are bad habits as the horse will not be straight and accepting the bit comfortably.

The outline of the horse should be one of roundness, the head and neck being carried so that the highest point is at the top of the poll. If the highest point is further down the neck it will mean that most of the weight is on the forehand with the croup being higher than the withers, showing that the horse has not been allowed or made to go forward truly from behind, before collection was asked.

As I have already stressed, it is vital that the potential dressage rider works very hard to develop a good deep and supple seat that is well-balanced. It is also important that the horse has good impulsion before collection otherwise none will be achieved. When the rider feels that he has achieved this, he must sit still, straighten his spine, maintaining the impulsion that he has created. The horse will lower his croup bending the three joints of the hindleg, the

Shandover during a Prix Caprilli at the Riding Club Championships

stifle, hip and hock, thus bringing them a little more under the body, and by the rider maintaining an elastic rein contact with the action of the rein going through the body, collection will be achieved. If collection is forced by resisting with the hand and sitting very heavily on the horse so that he hollows his back, the horse will be penalised. One often sees the trot shortened with the hindlegs not tracking up and the rhythm lost, and this is also incorrect. The horse should be able to maintain this good collected trot through all movements, though it is more difficult in turns and through corners. The rider must be aware of this and notice if the horse loses his rhythm when going through a corner. If he does it will mean that he is a little too heavy on the rider's hand or perhaps falling in in order to maintain his balance. If this happens then the horse is not truly collected and going forward. He is taking the easy way out by slowing up when coming to a corner, throwing his quarters in or out thus avoiding bending his hindleg, consequently the horse becomes crooked.

In my earlier chapter I have used the terms tempo, rhythm, cadence and forward movement. I would like to explain them a little more clearly to avoid confusion.

Tempo This can be defined as speed or the number of metres per minute covered within the movements of various paces. It is possible to lengthen or shorten the tempo. For example, in a class ride with several horses working together, one horse may slow down, going through the short end of the school thus changing his tempo, the whole ride previously working at the same tempo.

Rhythm This term describes the regularity of the paces at which the horse is working. A horse may have good rhythm, but not necessarily impulsion and cadence.

Cadence This is the manner in which the horse moves rhythmically, showing precision, elegance and brilliance of stride. It is impossible to have cadence without rhythm.

Forward movement A horse is said to be going freely forward, on all reins and in all paces, when his energy is coming from behind, and he seeks the rider's hand. Without this forward movement one cannot achieve any of the movements that we have discussed. To clarify this, a horse can have impulsion, but need not necessarily be collected. The race horse can gallop, the impulsive horse can move swiftly forward quickening his steps, a stallion in a herd of mares will show impulsion with excitement. Collection is like a spring; it is the impulsion compressed coming through the horse from behind, showing elevation, rhythm and cadence in every stride.

5 Riding a dressage test

The Pony Club tests, preliminary or novice tests

As you will have realised, dressage is simply training your horse to understand your aids or signals and to make it as easy as possible for him to carry your weight, so that life for him and you is fun. To be able to ride a dressage test well it is necessary to know how to design the movements, and in the following pages there are diagrams that I hope will help you in this matter. It is important that you really know your test. For pure dressage tests except at championships, selection trials or where stated on the schedule, you are now allowed to have it commanded, but you must still be so familiar with the test that you are able to concentrate on your horse and not on the actual design of movement. The basic movements required at the lower levels are the working paces, walk, trot and canter, with possibly a simple serpentine. In all tests you will be asked for transitions from working paces to halt and upwards; a twenty-metre circle at the rising or the sitting trot and perhaps at the canter. The preliminary is the easiest test, followed by the Pony Club tests and the BHS Novice tests. In these the judge is looking for the horse that is free and forward going, obedient and responsive to the rider's aids and with the impulsion coming from the hindquarters.

When learning the test it is a good idea to run on your own two feet through the test so that you are aware of the importance of accuracy and can have an idea of the pattern of the test whilst learning it. You may find it helpful to ride the test before the competition, although I am not keen on riders practising on the horse on which they intend to compete as the horse will begin to anticipate.

When your horse is well established in his basic paces going forward freely and reasonably obediently in the ordinary gaits, I think much can be gained by taking him to a small competition where he can receive experience competing at preliminary level.

It may be the first competition of this type for you as well as for your young horse so I hope that you will find the following hints helpful.

The day before the competition try to follow your normal routine as closely as possible so as not to upset your horse. Careful attention should be given to your turnout as I believe that if the horse and rider are looking their best and exceptionally neat and tidy the rider will feel much more confident to tackle the task in hand. Check your tack, cleaning it really well, looking at the stitching on the stirrup leathers and reins and ensuring that your buckles and girths are safe. You will also need for your horse a grooming kit, plaiting equipment, short feed, haynet, water in a container that is easy to carry, a bucket for feed and water, hoof oil and brush, travelling clothing that includes stable bandages, sweat rug, knee pads and tail bandage with tail guard and finally first aid equipment. This can be fairly basic but must include thermometer, colic drench, bandages, antiseptic powder and fly spray, the latter being very important, especially on a hot day as many marks can be lost by a horse that tosses its head when uncomfortable and worried by flies. Attention must also be given to your personal equipment. It is correct to wear gloves, which must be of a lighter colour, long boots, breeches, a hacking jacket or black jacket, stock or tie, with a bowler or hunting cap. A whip may be carried in novice tests, but not in Pony Club events, so if you require one this must also be put ready. When you progress to the more advanced tests, at medium level and above, you must wear a black coat. Both whips and spurs are permitted at all levels, but spurs are compulsory at medium and advanced. Before beginning your journey do

An immaculately turned-out pony performs a dressage exercise

Mortimer with Marie Stokes during a Ladies Hunter Class at The Royal International Horse Show. The Ladies Hunter must be pleasing to the eye and a joy to ride

remember to leave your horse's box or stall clean with a good deep bed, water and haynet, the rugs being hung to air and left neatly for his return. On arrival at the dressage meeting go to your horse and make sure that he has travelled well and is suffering from no injuries whatsoever. Next find the secretary's tent, declare your intention to ride and collect your numbers, find out in which arena you are to ride and if they are running to time, or perhaps a little behind time so that you will know how long to allow to ride your horse in. Do allow yourself plenty of time so that you are not rushed or flustered. If you have a friend who will travel with you and help then it is a good idea, as the friend may well help to keep you calm and relaxed. Your horse should have been fed before leaving his stable so do not feed him at the show until after his competition. It will do no harm, however, to remove the saliva and allow him to swallow a little clean water — in fact it will refresh him. I have already mentioned how important it is really to know your test. Do not try to learn it at the show; it is too late and you will only become hesitant and unsure of yourself. You should know the test so well that you feel fully confident and can convey that confidence to the horse. In pure dressage competitions it is now permissible to have the test commanded, but even so I repeat that it is still vital that you learn it in order that you can concentrate on riding the movements and the horse well rather than have to think about where you are going. In your riding-in period allow yourself time to relax, tidy yourself and polish the horse. It is a mistake to rush straight into the arena as soon as you are called; it is better to take a few deep breaths and smile so that you are relaxed and calm.

Although you may be inexperienced do not anticipate the results before you have competed because you could so easily be disappointed. The competition should be looked upon as a test of your horse's training so far. If you have a good ride and feel that you and your horse have both given of your best then the result is immaterial. Do take plenty of time. So often when one is judging one sees the junior competitor rushing down the centre line grinding to a halt, and then going full speed ahead to finish the test in the fastest possible time. Your entry and halt is very important as this first movement can give a good impression or mar the whole test. It is worth spending the time improving your entry and finish so that you show the judge an obedient and well-mannered horse. Should you make a mistake in your test try not to panic as you may spoil the next movement as well; remember that each movement is marked out of ten and if, for example, you know that you have spoilt a canter movement with a wrong strike off, relax, correct it as quickly as possible, and concentrate on riding the next movement really well. The preparation for each movement must be carried out in a calm manner, positioning your horse well and allowing plenty of time.

Your riding-in period before your test is also very important; try to do this quietly and in a relaxed manner, working your horse so that he is attentive to you, giving him the opportunity to relax in his back and joints and loosen up after his journey. When riding-in, work around the show ground allowing your horse to settle in the atmosphere and environment about him. The time that you allow to work your horse in will depend upon his temperament, experience and his degree of fitness or freshness. A horse with a very excitable temperament may need as much as 1½ hours to work in, on the other hand a horse of a more settled temperament may only require 20 minutes. It is only by competing and getting to know your horse that you will really discover what is the correct working-in period for him to enter the arena cool, calm, relaxed and able to perform a good test.

After your test do remember that your horse will have given of his best; dismount, slacken your girth and make much of him by giving him a titbit or a little grass. Next, take him back to your horsebox, remove all his tack and put on a headcollar. Your horse will probably want to stale, so do give him the opportunity; offer him a drink of water and let him have his short feed. Whilst he is

Shandover correctly tacked up with well fitting saddle and bridle for a novice test

An example of good breeding, portraying the elegance of the thoroughbred horse who is well suited for dressage

eating you can roll up his bandages, shake out his rugs and prepare his equipment generally for the homeward journey. Ask your friend to hold him whilst you take out his plaits and brush him off; this is only a quick groom to make him feel comfortable, removing any sweat from his saddle and bridle area. When this operation is completed he can be dressed with rugs and bandages etc. to travel. With your friend's help load him in the box or trailer. Now you may visit the refreshment tent and look at the scoreboard to see your mark — although the dressage sheets may not be collected until the competition has finished. When you receive your sheet do read it carefully; this is the time for reflection. From the judge's comments you will be able to note whether or not his observations compare with the problems of which you are already aware. Possibly the judge will have noticed something different; he may, for example, have spotted that your horse is not always straight, although perhaps you had not realised this. The judge's comments should give you something to go away and work on.

6 The aids

As yet, we have not properly discussed the prime means of communication between the horse and rider. This is by the aids, the means whereby the rider is able to convey his wishes to the horse. Initially the horse must be taught simple aids, the trainer clearly explaining what is required of the horse by the association of ideas. For example, the horse learns in the stable to move over when he is groomed by the trainer pressing his hand to the sides of the horse and saying 'Over'. Gradually the horse will learn to move away from the trainer's hand and consequently step over. Immediately the horse understands he should be rewarded with a pat or titbit. In teaching the horse the aids the rider is developing the horse's sense of hearing, sight and responsiveness to touch. It is this response to touch that the rider must most strive to develop, for with the advanced horse the chief means of communication will be by feel and the reactions of the horse to the rider's seat, leg and hand. There are several aids, the first being a driving or pushing aid, using the legs, the rider's weight, his voice, spurs and a long whip. The aids to slow down or stop are the rider's reins, back and the weight of the body. The good rider will have developed a good sense of feel and will therefore be able to anticipate and prevent an evasion occuring by the use of his legs in conjunction with his reins.

In the use of the aids you must learn to develop such co-ordination that you are able to use legs and hands independently of each other. Whereas with sports such as dancing, gymnastics or tennis the sportsman can use his arms to balance the rest of his body, one cannot when riding as to do so would cause the aids to become confused and muddled to the horse. To handle reins well with no interference or confusion to the horse is difficult and will only be achieved if the rider persists in improving the depth and independence of his seat. I am sure you have heard the expression 'good hands'. This does not mean that they are supple and attractive, but that they are sympathetic, effective and thus able to give the signals necessary to the horse for precision and control without the rider losing balance in any way. The simple aids are used diagonally. For example to turn to the right it is best to look to the right, placing your right leg at the girth with your left leg behind the girth, feeling in your right rein so that the horse is slightly bent to the right, your left rein, however, giving sufficiently to allow the horse to go to the right. When making any turn or change of direction it is important to look where you are going so that your own weight is in that direction. This way it will be easier for your horse to balance and oblige.

Transitions are a little more difficult. A transition is the change of pace or direction either from walk to trot, trot to canter, canter to trot or trot to walk. A transition should be smooth, fluid and forward going, the horse maintaining the rhythm and regularity of his stride. The secret of a good transition is to prepare the horse really well. Say to yourself the three little words, 'I have time', and in that time, think! Sit still, grow tall in the saddle; close both legs to rebalance your horse; resist a little with your hand and as soon as you feel the horse give to you lighten your hand and ride him forward. If not already, you will in time find that in the downward transition from trot to walk the horse loses impulsion. This is usually because, having asked for the downward transition, you were not quick enough to recover and lighten your hand, using the legs to send the horse energetically forward. Transitions are important both at the slow paces and the more energetic ones, and it is well worth your while practising them until you are able to ride them accurately and also maintain rhythm and balance. I cannot stress enough that the horse *must* go forward from behind in all that he does. The essence of all dressage tests is only to perform a series of movements at walk, trot, and canter, which is something that we do on any horse. This applies if one is competing at preliminary level or Grand Prix level. The only thing that alters is the amount of collection required at these three paces. For example, in a preliminary test no collection is asked for, but with years of training on correct lines this rhythmical pace can become *piaffe*. Therefore, if your syllabus of training has been thorough and on correct lines you should not have anything to worry about provided you have entered your horse in the correct test for his stage of training.

7 Prix Caprilli test

A competition becoming very popular is the Riding Club Prix Caprilli test for novice riders who are members of an affiliated Riding Club but have never competed in a two or three day event and have no senior professional qualifications. The horse ridden must also be a novice, never having won at an official meeting. This competition is most valuable for the young horse just starting out as it gives him a chance to compete and become used to shows and different environments, plus the fact that it is tremendous fun! The Prix Caprilli is a dressage test ridden from memory where the emphasis is on the rider's ability, co-ordination, control and style. The test includes two small fences of approximately two feet in height which are jumped from trot and canter, the emphasis here being on the fluent, well-balanced movement, also the ability to recover and put the horse on the correct lead after a fence, quickly and neatly. The competition is judged not on the performance of the horse but on the ability of the rider, the judge

Notice the good conformation of Master Pepé and the calmness of his outlook

looking for a good deep seat and accuracy and precision in riding. If you are competing in a Prix Caprilli and have trained your horse well so that he is obedient you will have a much easier ride, the horse complementing your seat so that you are able to achieve good results. Prix Caprilli competitions are sometimes held as closed Riding Club events, and sometimes open to all clubs. The Riding Club also organise an area trial where all the clubs in your area are invited to send a team to compete, the first two successful teams representing the area at Stoneleigh for the Riding Clubs' Prix Caprilli Final.

You may well decide to begin your young horse's dressage career by competing in Prix Caprilli competitions. I think they are excellent experience for both horse and rider. It can be quite an ordeal to ride down the centre line entering at the 'A' marker, see the judge's car straight ahead and realise that you are quite alone and that all the attention for the next few minutes is going to be on you and your horse.

In Prix Caprilli competitions you are not allowed to have the test commanded, so you must learn it really well to ride the movements without hesitation. A riding whip may be carried provided it is no longer than thirty inches, but spurs are not allowed. You will be required to jump two small fences in your test, so practise at home working your horse over trotting fences and low canter exercises; the emphasis being on the balance of your horse on landing. If your horse lands with a well-balanced stride it will be easier for you to ride your next movement accurately and it is worth spending a little time on this aspect. All of the movements are progressive with the horse moving through the transitions smoothly. Remember that the emphasis is not on your horse but on you — the rider. Transitions must be well prepared, the aids being applied positively and firmly; do not be in a hurry as it is not the object of the exercise to get through the test in the fastest possible time. Much can be gained by working on your entrance and finish. A good straight entry and halt with the horse standing squarely on all four legs is bound to give you good marks and create a good impression for your judge. If you are carrying a whip, place it in your left hand so that, when you have made your entry and halt, it is easy for you to perform the salute by putting both reins in your left hand and dropping your right hand by your side. Smile, it does help to relax your head and neck, and it is pleasant for the judge to feel that his time is not being wasted and that you are going to enjoy yourself.

In your move off, look forward to the track that you are going to take, making good preparation for the turn, remembering that the horse will very likely lose impulsion so a little more leg than usual is required. Diagonals are also important: when riding on the right rein, sit in the saddle on the left diagonal and vice versa for the other rein. It is not vital which diagonal you choose to ride on provided that you are consistent and remember to change according to the rein that you are on. I prefer the rider to sit on the outside diagonal as I think it is much more comfortable for the horse and enables him to balance better through his turns and circles. In making your transition to canter sit still, apply your aid with your inside leg on the girth and your outside one behind maintaining the flexion to the inside. Do not look down. So often one sees riders looking to see which lead they are on, dropping the contact of the inside rein, collapsing their own inside hip, and then wondering why the horse has struck off on the wrong lead. If you are uncertain of your leads it is well worth your while practising this; one of the first lessons that the rider must learn in order to develop feel. If you can get a friend to help you then so much the better. Ask your friend to tell you if you are on the wrong leg, shut your eyes and try to feel the movement underneath you and associate it with the corresponding strike-off. In canter left, if you shut your eyes, you should be able to feel that your own left hip and knee will seem a little in advance of the right one. Canter the movements slowly, the arena is not very large and you will find it easier to maintain your horse's balance at the slow paces. The exercise of the walk on a long rein or a loose rein is another movement where many marks are lost. Read your test carefully. If it clearly states a free walk on a loose rein then you must ride with the reins held at the buckle. If, however, it says on a long rein, then some contact must be maintained, the horse just being allowed to stretch down lowering its head and neck. The arena is forty metres long and twenty metres wide, therefore if you are asked to ride a circle of twenty metres at a given marker the circle must touch the track on all four sides at 'A' or 'C'. If the circle is to be in the centre, commenced at 'B' or 'E', then it will only touch the track on two sides. Prix Caprilli is very much an equitation event, so try to get some help with your riding. The seat must be deep and the aids quietly and firmly applied. The judge will be looking to see the depth of your seat, the co-ordination of your aids and their application, the effectiveness of your seat and the amount of control and precision that you are able to achieve with the movements required. A session on the lunge line would help to deepen your seat.

8 Hands

To ride well it is imperative that you give attention to your hands. It is often said that good hands are born and not made, but I think this is a debatable point and certainly believe that they can be improved if the interest and desire are there. Undoubtedly some people are born with lighter hands than others, but at least good hands may be acquired.

The rider must have a firm and independent seat, his knowledge of the art of horsemanship and technique must be thorough. Success will not be achieved, however, if the rider does not have control of his nerves and temper, maintaining a calm and sympathetic influence at all times with an understanding of the horse. Riding is an art first and a science second. The rider must first study the technique of handling the reins, the application of the aids and know the importance of a deep independent seat. When these points are understood and practised then riding becomes an art, the rider's position or attitude in the saddle should be natural and relaxed. To explain this a little more fully: the elbows should hang in a natural position, held loosely to the rider's side without constraint. The forearm should point obliquely across the body bringing the hands into an effective position, the elbows appearing heavy with the hands a fraction below the elbows. The thumbs must be on top of the rein and firmly closed, the wrists being

The rein back is a two-time movement

absolutely supple and relaxed, in a position that will be ready to give and take responding to the feelings from the horse's mouth. The fingers should be loosely closed around the rein, so that the horse will always know where your hand is, giving confidence at all times. A suitable length of rein will vary with each type of horse that you ride but a good guide is 'the longest possible rein compatible with the maximum amount of control'. It is important to realise that one's hands are valueless without the leg aids and the two must be used in conjunction with each other.

Good hands are also dependent upon your temperament and nerves, your sympathy and skill. Your ability to anticipate the actions of the horse is also important, coupled with the knowledge of how to deal with them. By riding many different horses and studying their likes, dislikes, temperament and peculiarities, you should be able to develop a greater sense of feel and tact. When I talk of sympathy and tact with horses, I am referring to the ability to anticipate the character and feelings of the horse, thus enabling him to cope with the subsequent reactions that may occur in his mouth and paces. Riding is dependent upon technique and guile, always try to work your young horse in an environment that will enable you to finish on a good note. It is a bad policy to school at a show or out hunting, in fact under any circumstance that is likely to upset or disturb him. When the horse has been well-schooled at home and going forward to a contact between the rider's hand and leg, then that is the time to ask questions of him and show or hunt him.

The action of the hands   The hands, through the reins and the bit in the horse's mouth, control and receive the energy and impulsion produced by the legs. It is also the purpose of the hands to direct and control the head, neck and shoulders of the horse. By opposing the shoulders to the hindquarters it is also possible for the horse just to move his quarters. The hands have three prime functions; they act, resist and yield, such as when riding a transition to halt, or making a left or right turn. When riding at the collected paces the hand will resist, but in jumping or when the horse has worked well and the riding is on a long rein the hand should yield.

When your seat is well established you should be able to use the reins with sympathy, to give and take, being quick to anticipate and quick to react, but never more strongly than is necessary to influence the horse. A good guide is that the hands should form a straight line from the elbow through to the rein. When competing in Prix Caprilli competitions special attention should be given to hands, seat, and application of the aids.

9 The main points of judging, and how to ride a better test

When you have taken part in your first competitions you will be able to learn from the judges' observations. The judge will have been impartial whilst noting down his opinions on that day. There will be occasions when the judges' opinions seem to differ. This is natural and should not alarm you even though at times it can be a little depressing! If you are to enjoy riding dressage tests competitively, be satisfied if your horse gives you a good ride, read your sheet carefully and where you have lost marks work to see if you can improve the horse in that respect. I hope my observations in the following paragraphs may help any potential dressage judges among you as well as the competitor!

The most common way of judging is to use a points system where the test is divided into movements, each of which is allocated a total of ten marks. The result is assessed by adding all the marks together to give a plus score.

The dressage judge must have an eye for beauty, taking in the whole picture that the horse creates in front of him. Naturally he

Riding a corner

The horse must be bent in the direction of his travel

is observing the technical merits of the movements and will hope to see in front of him a horse that is free and forward going, responsive to the rider's aids, working accurately and obediently, with the impulsion coming from the hindquarters through to the forehand. This must be your aim as a rider and competitor — to train your horse so well that he shows this lightness and elegance in his paces.

In the walk the rider may find difficulty in maintaining the rhythm of the pace showing the freedom and energy demanded. The judge will be looking to see if the horse is completely straight and responsive to the rider's aids; whether or not the hindlegs are active so that the walk is diligent and purposeful. If you feel that your walk is fast it may not be correct. The horse must move forward symmetrically with the power coming from behind. When working at the trot it is important that you are able to follow the movements of the extended and collected paces very closely. If the seat is not sufficiently deep the trot will suffer and the rhythm and cadence will very likely be lost. Here again the judge will be looking for straightness, rhythm, accuracy and impulsion. It is a common fault in trot for the horse to swing his quarters to the outside, so this is something that you must be aware of in the schooling of your horse, as it will be heavily penalised in a competition. In the canter work the judge is again looking for straightness — the inner front foot in front of the inner hind foot; the horse's back should be round and swinging showing the rider sitting in the saddle relaxed and close to the horse at all times. Sometimes, particularly with spirited horses, the canter will be seen to be on two tracks with the hindquarters coming on the inner track; this will mean that the horse is not straight and must be considered as a serious fault. In the strike-off to canter the aids should be almost impossible to see, the transition being made calmly and fluently. All transitions made from one pace to another, and those within the pace, such as collected trot to extended trot, should be carried through smoothly and positively showing plenty of impulsion. A rough transition shows lack of balance and possibly poor preparation for the movement. When making a transition it is important that the horse is listening and attentive to his aids, and is given a well-prepared and positive signal. When riding a corner the horse must be bent in the direction of his travel maintaining the same tempo throughout the whole movement. If the corner is taken too fast the hindquarters may fall out, losing the impulsion and with the horse failing to maintain the purity of pace. Circles must be circles! A circle has no corners! How often one sees a shape that is supposed to represent a circle, yet is square or looks like an egg! In a good circle the horse is bent throughout his whole length, the circle being an exact shape with the horse tracking up, meaning that the horse is straight with the hindlegs following into the same footfalls of the corresponding forelegs. The serpentine, when correctly ridden, should be a fluid movement with the horse maintaining the bend respectively for each loop. The horse will be straight with the hindlegs following the tracks of the forelegs. It goes without saying, of course, that the loops must be of the prescribed size and the rhythm of the pace maintained.

Riding Club Team of three working in unison at the White City

10 Transport

Dressage competitions are very widespread throughout the country, so if you become an enthusiast and wish to compete extensively it may be necessary for you to travel long distances, sometimes staying overnight. It is important, therefore, that your horse **becomes accustomed to being transported and is relaxed and** undisturbed by the loading into the vehicle or the actual journey. You would be well advised to teach a young horse to load at home long before you wish to take him on a journey, either by feeding him in the trailer or by loading another horse first and letting him follow. Take him for a short drive for about five minutes only so that he realises there is nothing to fear. You may not, however, have your horse as a youngster and may have to teach him to load easily as a grown and mature horse. Here are some pointers on loading for the inexperienced handler.

a   Position the horse box or trailer next to a hedge or in a gateway

Dressed for a journey

Loading in
a trailer

A well-trained horse who has confidence in his trainer creates no problem when loading

where a natural wing will be provided. Place the ramp on an incline so that the angle of entry to the trailer is slight.

b Have a feed and haynet ready, open the windows and ventilators for more light. You will also need a lunge line or rope and an assistant.

c Put a headcollar on the horse with a bridle on top. The horse should be dressed with travelling equipment consisting of a tail bandage, stable bandages, knee boots, and a rug.

d Walk confidently in a straight line to the box, being careful not to hesitate or rush the horse; try to remain close to his shoulder without looking back, or getting in front of him.

e Having walked with the horse right inside the box, ask your assistant to attach the rear strap quickly so that the horse does not reverse smartly back out of the box. Next, tie up the horse, removing the bridle at the same time. Allow the horse sufficient room to eat his hay, but little enough that he is not able to turn round or bite his neighbour!

Sometimes you may meet a horse that is reluctant to load and the following hints may be helpful to you in that instance.

a A nervous horse who will not look at the box or even approach it is a problem. You must take your time and never try to load this type of horse if you yourself are in a hurry as you will only frighten the horse more. Encourage him with a feed, handling him firmly and quietly; if possible put the horse in long reins and drive him into the box. If the horse is fully encased between the trainer and the reins, and you have an efficient assistant to do up the backstrap quickly when you are in the box, you will find that this method is nearly always successful.

b Another type of problem you may have is with the horse who stands at the edge of the ramp and will go no further, swinging his quarters and jumping off the ramp. When you have the horse standing quietly in front of the ramp, take a lunge line behind him, placing it above the hocks and under the tail, wearing gloves; with gentle pressure on the line the horse should move away and go forward into the box. If this does not work, try loading another horse first and perhaps the difficult horse will follow.

Try regularly loading the horses that are difficult to handle, feeding them in the box when it is stationary, so that they begin to treat the box as though it were another stable. The driver should be careful to give the horse as comfortable a ride as possible, changing gear often, using all the gears, driving slowly, especially on corners. It is stupid to give the horse a valid reason to be afraid of the box. You may think this a strange subject to have included in a book about dressage, but I consider it a very important subject. If your horse is worried about loading, or the journey, he will very likely become tense and excited, unsettling himself so that it is impossible for you to ride him calmly. A journey is quite tiring for you, so remember that it is also tiring on your horse and if you wish to do well, see that he is driven well and carefully, allowing plenty of time.

Right. Here one sees the strength of the Riding Club movement. The Team of Three Class at the Royal International Horse Show. The riders are required to give a dressage display as a team working in unison, notice how the team in action appear to be moving as one

11 Equipment and saddlery for the competition horse

The saddle that you use should be so shaped that it encourages you to sit in its central and lowest part. A full panel model is best as there is less chance of the saddle slipping thus making the horse uncomfortable. The fitting of the saddle is vital as a badly fitting saddle is often the reason for the horse not being able to give of his best. The weight of the saddle must be evenly distributed on the lumbar muscles leaving the loins free. A clear channel should be easily visible along the horse's spine, this having no weight upon it even with a rider mounted. The front arch of the saddle must fit the horse so that there is no pressure on the wither or to either side of the wither. If the pommel is narrow the wither will be pinched and the horse subjected to pain. From time to time it will be necessary for you to have the saddle re-stuffed because constant wear will cause the padding to become thin, consequently the saddle will press down on the horse and possibly make him sore. It is a good practice to have the saddle re-stuffed and the stitching checked once a year. In novice tests an ordinary snaffle is used and for elementary and above a simple double bridle may be used. Artificial aids such as martingales and bearing, side or running reins are all forbidden, as are over-reach boots, brushing boots and bandages. A whip may be carried in preliminary or novice tests but not in Pony Club or Horse Trials Group tests; in the higher tests a whip is not allowed although one should wear spurs. Failure to wear spurs in tests of medium standard and above could result in elimination from the contest.

The British Horse Society at the National Equestrian Centre, Stoneleigh, Kenilworth, Warwickshire, publish a booklet of *The*

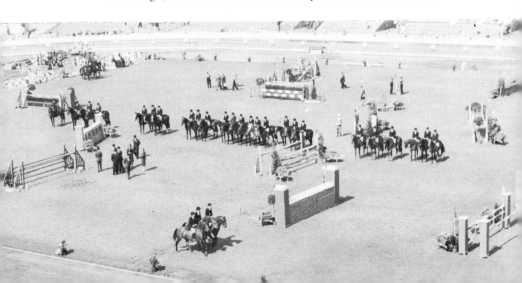

official rules for dressage and the correct procedure for competitions. The booklet gives the sizes of the novice arena and the advanced arena, includes rules for combined competitions and advice on the interpretation of the dressage test sheets. It also quotes some extracts from the Official FEI Rules as applied to dressage competitions.

If you wish to compete in official competitions either for dressage or combined training then it is necessary to become a member of the British Horse Society's Dressage Group and also the Combined Training Group and register your horse. By becoming a member of the Society you have the advantage of being kept fully up-to-date with any new rules and tests, and you will also be informed of the venues of all dressage competitions that are affiliated to the Society. If you have problems, either in receiving instruction, interpreting the rules as they apply to you or any other matter which applies to dressage, the dressage group will help you if they possibly can, and certainly let you know where assistance can be obtained. So I strongly advise that you become a member of the Society.

Shoulder-in　　Below left. The first beginnings being made from a small circle
Below right. Showing the position of the horse in relation to the fence

12 Further movements to assist training and more advanced work

Shoulder-in This is a most important exercise that the horse must learn quite early in his training. It is an athletic exercise that will improve the suppleness of the horse in his back, stifle, hip and hocks. The shoulder-in is a movement in which the horse's inner feet step in front of the outer feet, the horse being bent around the rider's inside leg. The horse must maintain the purity of the trot, moving forward with **well-established** and rhythmical steps. In the shoulder-in the horse is moving forwards and sideways, the forehand coming a little off the track whilst the quarters remain on the track. The angle that the horse makes in relation to the track should be no more than 30 degrees with the horse bent to the inside. Shoulder-in is one of the two movements in which the horse is not bent in the direction of his travel. The aids for the shoulder-in are diagonal, the horse being asked to go from the rider's inside leg to take the outside rein. If one thinks of the horse forming a segment of a circle, the shoulder-in becomes an extension of that circle. To

Shoulder-in Progressing out of the corner, maintaining an angle of 30° with the horse bent to the inside

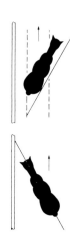

Left. Right shoulder-in lateral movement in which the horse is not bent in the direction of his travel.

Below left. *Travers* on lateral movement in which the quarters move to the inner track with the horse looking the direction of his way of going.

begin shoulder-in, work the horse first in collected trot, using small circles of approximately 10 metres. When you feel that the impulsion is good and the horse listening to you bent in the direction of his circle, you can then ask him to increase the size of his circle by going on to a slightly larger circle using shoulder-in. As I have already said, the aids are diagonal, so if, for example, you are working on the left rein, I suggest that you commence your circle in the corner of the school. Ride at the sitting trot, as you come through the corner of the school making the arc of the circle using the inside leg actively on, or a little to the rear of, the girth, the inside rein maintaining the flexion left. The outside or right rein controls speed, being used as a direct open rein asking the horse to go from your inside leg and take the outside rein. If you are careful to look in the direction that you wish to go, you should find that you have the beginnings of shoulder-in. Sometimes the movement may be unbalanced and hurried with the horse falling on to his outside shoulder. Ask for just a few steps at a time and ride the horse forward on to a circle and rebalance;

Below left. Left shoulder-in begun from 10 metre circle
Below right. *Travers* begun from small circle

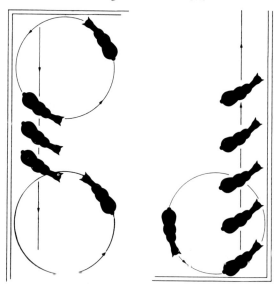

Demi-pirouette

when the trot is re-established, ask for the movement again. It goes without saying that the horse must be trained equally on both reins, the shoulder-in being the foundation for all other lateral movements. Before beginning any lateral work the horse must move forward and straight using himself correctly on the single track.

The shoulder-in is used mainly as an exercise for schooling the horse, improving his athletic ability and making him more supple through his back. As the tests become more difficult shoulder-in may be asked for; it appears as a definite movement in the medium level tests and in some elementary tests, although at elementary level only a few steps will be requested. In the following pages I have included diagrams to give a better idea of the plan to the correct entry for the lateral movements. Master Pepé, our model for this book, is also working in shoulder-in and I hope that you can see from the photographs the obvious impulsion that he has compressed in his rhythmical and cadenced steps.

Travers Here again the horse is bent in his longitudinal form; the outside legs step in front of the inside legs. The horse should be moving forward with impulsion, looking in the direction he is going. *Travers* is sometimes known as quarters-in, as what happens in effect is that the rider holds the forehand on the track with both reins, the outside rein having a slightly firmer contact than the inside. The outside leg is supporting the hand and asking the quarters to move to the inside, whilst the inside leg in the normal position at the girth allows the horse to go forward and ensures the correct position of the head and neck, keeping the lateral bend in the horse's body. This type of work will increase the activity of the hindquarters and improve the horse in suppleness if it is correctly performed. Ask for just a few steps to begin; put the quarters back on the track and ride the horse forward before asking again. It is a mistake to ask for too much at a time, thus encouraging the horse to move crookedly rather than really use himself.

Stephen Clark on Warlock's Wager at Stoneleigh in 1987 — something to aspire to

Renvers This is another exercise that will improve the **obedience** of the horse and make him more supple throughout his joints. In *renvers* the quarters stay on the track with the tail to the wall, the horse maintaining the bend of the direction of his travel. The aids are as follows. You must ask for just a little to begin with, being careful to maintain the tempo and the impulsion. The horse is ridden forward by your seat and legs, the outside leg being on the girth is the most active, keeping the lateral bend and the outline of the horse. The inside leg used a little behind the girth should ask the horse to step forward and sideways. If the exercise falls unbalanced, ride the horse forward beginning again with the small collected trot circles before **asking** for any more.

Demi-pirouette This is a turn of 180 degrees normally ridden in the school with the rider asking the horse to bring his forehand round to describe a small circle around the hindquarters. In effect, therefore, it is a half-turn on the haunches. The forehand begins the half-turn describing a semi-circle round the haunches, without hesitating, at the moment the inside hindleg stops moving forward. The horse should commence forward movement again, smoothly without

52

Counter-canter   The horse in counter-canter

hesitation when the half-turn is completed. In a *demi-pirouette* to
the right the horse will be bent to the right, the forehand becoming
lighter and the horse lowering his croup. To ride a *demi-pirouette*
the aids are as follows: the outside leg is behind the girth, the
inside leg on the girth, the inside hand is a direct opening rein
asking the horse to take that rein, the outside rein controls the
amount of the turn and regulates the speed. Before a good
pirouette can be achieved the horse must first be working in the
collected paces well and maintaining good impulsion. This exercise
of the *demi-pirouette* is very valuable as it encourages the horse to
lighten his forehand, lower his croup and bring his weight back.
From a good pirouette the hindlegs should be well engaged and
the horse beautifully positioned, therefore, to spring forward into
canter. This movement is a good test of the horse's obedience and
training, showing his ability and response to the aids. It is best
taught at the walk, by using a corner of the school, entering the
corner and asking for the pirouette leading the forehand with the
inside rein. The horse should find it easy to step round making a
half-turn and proceed forward on the opposite rein.

Counter-canter   This is a 'false' canter, by which I mean that if you are cantering to the right then the left leg will be leading, the horse flexed to the left. The counter-canter is an important exercise in the training of the horse: it is a test of his obedience, athletic ability, suppleness and balance. The aids for the counter-canter are the opposite to those of the normal canter. The inside leg is placed behind the girth and requests the movement, whilst the outside leg remains close to the barrel of the horse in the normal position and asks for the actual strike-off, helping to maintain the bend to the leading leg. The outside rein directs the horse and maintains the bend to the outside, preventing the shoulder from coming in and otherwise making the horse go crookedly. The inside rein acts as a balance rein limiting the position to the outside and helps maintain the direction of the horse's way of travel and speed. The movement of counter-canter must be smooth and fluid, just as calm and fluid as that of the ordinary canter. There should be no change in your seat or loss of balance. You should sit still and straight with your hip a little forward to the direction of the leading leg.

Counter-canter should be introduced to the horse gradually, when he is well-established in his ordinary canter and balanced on both

Renvers   Here the hindquarters stay on the track, the horse maintaining the bend of the direction of his travel

reins. Begin by riding a shallow loop on the long side of your school or manège, then make it a little deeper always maintaining the bend to the direction of the leading leg. From the shallow loop ride a large *demi-volte* of approximately fifteen metres on returning to the track walk. When the horse can do this on both reins commence the exercise of the *demi-volte* again, but this time ask the horse to hold his canter for a few strides through the corner of the school. When the horse is able to canter through the short end of the school in counter-canter then proceed to a figure of eight and hold the canter throughout the complete movement. Finally, you should both be able to produce counter-canter up the centre line of the school or manège.

The half-pass This is another movement on two tracks where the horse moves obliquely forward. There is a slight flexion in the horse's head and neck to the direction of his way of travel. In the half-pass the horse should move forward obliquely as I have described with the position of his body parallel with the long side of the manège or school; the quarters must not come in advance of the forehand, and on reaching the track the horse should arrive to the track straight. In a dressage test, the judges would mark the movement with a fault if the hindquarters were leading.

The easiest way to ride this movement is to begin at the collected trot (easier in trot to maintain forward impulsion) by turning down the centre line of the arena. At 'A' or 'C' continue to ask the horse to go forward with plenty of impulsion obliquely onwards to the track. If, for example, you are on the left rein, turn left at 'A' and ask for left half-pass. This way the horse will be well positioned before commencing the movement. In a good half-pass the horse should be bent in his longitudinal axis, with the rhythm and cadence maintained. There should be no sign of the hindquarters leading or a twisting in the head and neck. Viewed from the front, the horse's head should be in a slightly raised position with both ears level.

13 Training the young horse

I began this book by explaining to you the meaning of the word dressage. So you will realise by now that dressage means the training and development of athletic ability of the horse to carry the rider with the least fatigue, the greatest ease and from which the lightest control can result. The prime principles of dressage that should be kept firmly in one's mind are that the horse must go calmly forward and straight. These first lessons are best begun and established when the horse is still unbroken.

The trainer must strive to gain the confidence of the horse, by kindness, patience and observation. Each horse that is trained will develop its own character, but the aim of the trainer with every horse must be to develop the horse's physical powers, making him quiet to ride, responsive, and able to balance himself with the weight of the rider upon his back.

The first stage Begin by fitting a cavesson on the horse with a lunge rein attached. You should lead the horse about on either side, frequently stopping, handling him and using the voice to get him accustomed to voice and touch. All of the early lessons should be given in a quiet place where the horse will have no distractions. When the horse leads quietly in hand and will stop, walk on and halt in the cavesson, then the time has come to put an ordinary snaffle bit in the horse's mouth. This bit must be fitted carefully for comfort and to discourage him from getting his tongue over the bit.

The second stage When the horse walks well in hand the time has come to begin lunge lessons. First, the horse must be correctly tacked up with boots on all four legs to prevent injury that could result if he lost his balance when learning. Lungeing will help to strengthen his muscles, bringing him into condition and teaching him obedience. On the lunge, the horse becomes accustomed to your voice and responds to it for walk, trot, canter and halt. For the slow paces speak slowly; for trot and canter however, speak a little more sharply to achieve a result. The horse responds well to the tone of the voice. After the first two or three days a lunge roller may be fitted and also the bridle with a pair of side reins fitted loosely. The side reins are fitted to give the horse a little support, giving him something to go to, remembering, of course, that the impulsion comes from behind and that the horse must be asked from the beginning to seek a contact. The horse should be worked on the lunge for four to six weeks before rider or saddle are introduced.

Above left. Half-pass to the left, the horse moving forwards and sideways

Above right. Half-pass to the right – the horse is looking to the right moving forwards and sideways

When the horse is working confidently with the lunge roller firmly in position and responds well to the voice, then the time has come to fit a saddle. It is advisable to fit a surcingle on top of the saddle to prevent its slipping back and frightening the horse. When introducing anything new to the horse, speak to him, reassure him so that he realises there is no cause to be frightened. When the horse is working well at all paces on the lunge with a saddle on he is ready to be mounted.

The third stage *Mounting*

This should be done in an enclosed space after the horse has been well worked. You will need an assistant, who must be someone of a light weight, reasonably efficient as a rider and certainly quiet and unafraid. Any tension that your assistant may show will quickly be transferred to your young horse. The trainer stays on the ground, as by now the horse should have good confidence in him. The rider should first lie across the saddle and make much of the horse. This should be done on both sides and it is a good idea to walk the horse a few steps so that he becomes accustomed to the extra weight, remembering that to begin with he will have difficulty in balancing. When the horse is relaxed and confident with the assistant across his back he should be brought to a halt for the rider to dismount and make much of the horse. The assistant should mount again by receiving a leg up, first lying across the horse, high towards neck, then keeping low on the horse bring the right leg over to be astride, sitting still and patting him, talking all the time. It is a good idea for the horse to wear a neck strap so that there is no risk of the rider hanging on by the reins.

The first mounted lessons
These early lessons should be spent teaching the horse to go forward, first at the walk and then at the trot. Ride transitions to halt, practise mounting and dismounting on both sides. The trainer should lunge the horse to begin with, with the rider mounted, using the voice to encourage the horse to move forward. From the very early mounted lessons the young horse must be taught to respond to the rider's leg, as the basis of all equitation is free forward movement. In training the horse a definite aid must be given with the legs used by making vibrations to the sides of the horse in the girth area. The voice may also be used to begin with, to reassure the horse and ask him to move forward. The first lessons should all take place in an enclosed space, for short periods only. The young horse may tire very quickly, so the trainer must be careful not to overtax him by working for too long. The horse may now begin work off the lunge line, but preferably after first being worked without the rider to give him the opportunity to relax in his back. The horse will benefit from working on good straight lines being ridden energetically forward at the walk, trot, and into halt; a few turns and large circles may be commenced, with the rider maintaining a light contact on the reins.

The next period of training This should be devoted to making the horse understand more complicated aids, continuing the work on large circles, making transitions and changes of direction. Teach the horse to turn on the forehand, progress from here to canter, beginning first by riding a small trot circle and coming out of the circle riding forward to canter. Alternatively, ask the horse to canter by following another horse up a gentle slope in a field where there are no other distractions. It does not matter at this stage if the horse falls a little into canter; do not worry if he goes on the wrong leg, but bring him quietly back to trot and ask again. When the horse is responding quietly to the simple aids it is a good idea to commence hacking through country lanes with an older and more experienced horse. This session of training should take place over a period of about six months during the first year after the horse has been backed. I think it is a good idea to back the horse as a three-year-old, turn him away to mature until he is a four-year-old, and then work him on the sort of lines that I have already explained. In his fifth year the horse must be taught to flex, accepting the bit and responding to your leg aids and going forward into a contact. Lateral movements at the walk and trot may be begun, teaching the horse to change leads by a simple change of leg at the canter. Practise working quietly over small fences. In all of this work the trainer must ask for vigorous impulsion to come from behind, this being the essence of good training and free forward movement. Much can be gained by riding the horse across country at all paces, both in company and alone, a type of work which teaches the horse to balance himself and should make him a safe performer over all kinds of country.

If your early work has been thorough, your horse should by the end of his fifth year be fairly well trained in the fundamentals of simple dressage. The horse should stand still for mounting and

Lungeing Lungeing is an exercise enabling the rider to improve her seat

dismounting and have the ability to lead well in hand with fluent paces. His balance should be developed to his stage of training to such a degree that he has 'self carriage'. Obviously the horse must be obedient to the correct aids. I hope that in your hacking you will have accustomed the horse to traffic and unusual sights and sounds and have ensured that he responds to the leg so well that he will go alone in company at any pace required without pulling and pull up quickly and smoothly when required.

In the training of your young horse I would like you to use my notes only as a guide. Every horse with which you come into contact will have a different temperament and problems. The fundamentals to remember are to keep calm and relaxed yourself, adhering as far as possible to a definite programme. This way both you and your horse should make good progress.

I have outlined below a suggested simple syllabus of training for your young horse, stressing that it is intended only as a guide.

First stage, approximately three months

First month. Accustom the horse to the surroundings by leading him about in his environment, allowing him to see and hear strange sights and sounds.

Second month. Work the horse on the lunge at walk and trot. Teach the horse to answer to the voice.

Third month. Work on the lunge in trot. Prepare horse to receive a rider on his back by making much of him. Work the horse mainly on straight lines, increase and decrease pace to supple him through his back and loins. Progress to working the horse over small fences from trot and canter.

Second stage, approximately three months

The horse should now be working on turns and circles, cantering large circles and straight lines. Begin lateral work, progressing on to turn on the haunches, rein back, cantering on a named leg, and *demi-pirouette.* In this latter stage the horse should be performing lateral movements at trot and canter, the aim being perfection achieved by repetition. Ride across country.

Summary of expressions used

As with any specialized subject, particular phrases are often used to explain a movement, in a context that applies to that subject and therefore not always clearly understood. In the following paragraphs I have tried to explain some of the expressions that you may meet in the course of your studies.

Aids — Aids are the signals by which the rider conveys his wishes to the horse. They form a common language between horse and rider.

Free forward movement — The stage at which the horse is willing to go forward at all paces at all times at his rider's command.

Disunited — Where, at the canter, the sequence has changed either in front or behind and the canter becomes false.

Balance — A horse is said to be balanced when the weight of the rider and horse is evenly distributed to such effect that the horse can use himself with maximum ease and efficiency.

Rhythm — Is the way the horse moves. He should move forward rhythmically and smoothly.

Cadence — Cadence is the rhythm of stride; the beat or timing of stride.

Contact — This is the rein that is held taut from the rider's hand to the bit. The rein is stretched, the lightness and firmness of the contact will vary with each rider and horse.

Tension — The lightness of contact coupled with firmness and support taken by the horse on the reins.

Half-halt — An exercise to rebalance the horse and lighten his forehand bringing him to attention.

Above the bit — The horse carries his head too high with the bit operating on the corners of the lips instead of the bars of the mouth.

Behind the bit — The horse bringing the angle of his face behind the perpendicular and consequently dropping the bit.

Suspension — This is the moment when the horse is suspended with all four legs in the air, when working at the trot.

Lateral work — Here the horse moves forward and sideways.

Calmness — Comes from stability of balance and the understanding of requirements and the ability to carry them out.

Unconstrained — Elastically contracting and relaxing the muscles more or less energetically, e.g. on a loose rein.

Sloppy running — Unbalanced owing to poor weight distribution.

Straightness – The horse working forward correctly with the hindlegs following into the same track of the corresponding forelegs.

Tracking up – This also means that the horse is straight and that the hindlegs follow into the same steps as the forelegs through all paces.

Forward – This must not be confused with speed. It is the will or urge to move forward, the development of the thrust of the hindquarters, the lengthening of stride and suppleness of back muscles, the impulsion coming from behind.

Tempo – Is the speed of the number of metres per minute covered within the movements of the various paces.

Dishing – The lower part of the foreleg that is below the knee is carried outwards as the horse goes forward at the trot.

Overbent – When the chin of the horse is almost touching the windpipe.

Stargazing – Another bit evasion, when the horse puts his nose so far forward that he cannot see the ground immediately in front.

Poking the nose – With this evasion the horse does not bend correctly at the poll.

Nappy – Said of a horse that refuses to go forward.

Tail swishing – In a dressage test a horse will lose marks if perpetually throwing his tail from side to side.

Resisting – When the horse is not accepting the bit; he will open his mouth and raise his head.

Unbalanced – The unbalanced horse is one not able to carry himself without the support of the rider's hand.

Lacking activity – Descriptive of a horse who seems rather flat and idle in his paces, showing very little impulsion.

Forging – When the toe of the hind shoe strikes the underneath surface of the corresponding front shoe.

Brushing – Here the horse's opposite limbs hit one another alternately, normally on the fetlock. Sometimes, however, it may be the coronet.

Conformation: notes on a suitable horse to buy

If you are thinking of buying a horse for dressage, showing or competition work of any sort, you are well advised first to consider the horse as a whole, taking in his good and bad points. In the next paragraphs I will enlarge upon some of these and discuss their relevant importance.

For dressage one seeks a quality horse, so when first viewing a horse for sale, look at him standing in the stable. In a quality horse one hopes to see a small head well set on with a good, big eye, a deep girth with plenty of room for the heart and lungs. The horse should be well coupled with his hocks well let down, the quarters being strong and the tail nicely set on. The feet are very important and must be of a good shape, the legs having plenty of bone in proportion to the frame of the horse. It is a pleasure to see a fine coat, rich in colour, the mane and tail also very fine in texture. The quality horse will be the owner of small chestnuts and ergots, the overall picture being one of superiority and refinement. It goes without saying that the horse must be sound both in wind and limb, with no vices, such as kicking, crib-biting, windsucking, rearing or weaving. When trotted out in hand the horse must move with a fluent, straight and true action.

The impression should be one of a horse in healthy condition throughout, a good looker, kind in temperament and, of course, sensible. Ideally the horse should be traffic-trained and if possible should be a good performer in summer and winter.

A point that I consider particularly important is the length of the horse's back. It is a mistake to buy a horse that is very long or very short in the back, as either way there will be difficulty with the extended and the collected paces. The horse should have a good, deep girth with solid quarters tapering to a gentle slope. The neck must be well set on to a good pair of gradually sloping shoulders. Every type of horse can be improved by correct dressage training, but the better the conformation of the horse the greater the results that will be achieved. The perfect horse does not exist, so one must be prepared to accept certain faults. If the cannon bone is a little long for the dressage horse this does not really matter. It does, however, matter if the horse is cow-hocked with his toes turned in or out as this will spoil the paces. A horse that is very thick through the throat will also be a problem — this type finding it much more difficult to relax the jaw and often running on the forehand, finding it very difficult to become light. The thoroughbred makes an ideal dressage horse, possessing the elegance and presence required in the more advanced

tests. In this book are photographs of two very different types, both successful in the dressage world. The first, that I have already mentioned, is Master Pepé, a Swedish-bred horse very well coupled together, showing a nice depth of girth, a well set on head and neck with beautiful hindquarters. Master Pepé demonstrates very clearly that with good training a horse develops the ideal outline, being really fit with his muscles firm and well developed. I think you will also agree that he shows tremendous athletic ability, able to carry his rider with little fatigue and with the greatest ease from which the lightest control can result. The calmness of his outlook comes from the stability of balance, an understanding of what is required of him, and the ability to carry it out. The other horse was bred to race, has chased very successfully, and now in his more gracious years has applied himself well to the art of dressage. His conformation is magnificent; he has a good length of back with a nice depth of girth, a well set on head and neck with a good sloping shoulder. He is a thoroughbred horse, a sophisticated breed of elegance and beauty showing true lightness in his paces which is the essence of artistic equitation. Without these two horses I could not have begun to write this book. Having had the opportunity to ride and watch them work, I have been able to study paces, impulsion and movement; the horse always being the schoolmaster.

A good dressage horse, in addition to correct conformation, must be intelligent and have a calm temperament. In this picture, Shandover and Master Pepé express these qualities

14 Making a dressage arena

A dressage arena may be one of two sizes only. For Preliminary, Novice and Elementary standards the required size is 20 by 40 metres, and it is in this sort of arena that I will expect most of my readers to be working. However, at the more advanced levels the arena size is 20 by 60 metres, to accommodate the more intricate and advanced work.

When making your own arena try to find a piece of ground that is **level and as far away from the general public as possible.** If you are organising a One-Day Event where you have dressage, show-jumping, and cross-country it is absolutely essential to ensure that the jumping areas are not close to the dressage arenas. Nothing is more annoying than to have left home at the crack of dawn with a young horse to find that the dressage is situated next to the jumping arena, with the result that the horse is distracted and only a poor mark achieved.

An arena may be marked either by a continuous surround of white boards or by the use of intermittent boards which are placed at each corner and opposite each marker. If this is not possible then it is in order to paint a white line on the ground, though if this method is used then the corners should have white posts 1 metre high. The centre line from A to C is best shown by a mown strip about 80 cm wide, as I consider that the method of making a white line down the centre or using sawdust is very distracting for the novice horse in his first competitions.

The markers should be shown clearly around the outer edge of the arena, displayed in black and white and placed about 2 metres from the outer edge. The centre markers G, X, L and D should be shown by sawdust or whitening. The A marker is best placed 3 metres away from the outer edge, leaving an entrance of 2 metres to allow all the horses to make a good, straight entry and beginning to their test. In the later pages you will see that I have shown two diagrams of the dressage arenas, the first a 20 by 40-metre Novice arena and the second being the advanced arena of 20 by 60 metres.

Jennie Loriston-Clarke, top British dressage rider. Correct turnout for advanced competitions includes double bridle, spurs, top hat and swallowtail coat.

15 Understanding and interpreting the dressage tests

Many readers may find the tests as presented and published by the British Horse Society a little puzzling to follow and understand until they have had the opportunity to watch, ride, and read several tests. In the next few pages, by using diagrams with explanations, I hope to make the tests easier to watch and ride.

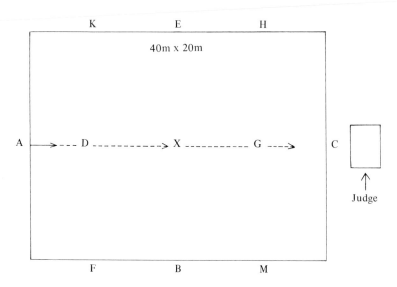

A Enter at working trot
X Halt, salute, proceed at working trot.

Explanation

The competitor enters at the A marker in the working trot and proceeds to X where he halts, and salutes the judges who are in a car behind the C marker. This is the first test of obedience and training, and although it is natural for the horse to wish to rest one or other of his hind legs, he is required at X to stand absolutely still and square on all four legs. After saluting the judges – and, of course, remembering to smile – the competitor moves off at the working trot.

THE ADVANCED ARENA

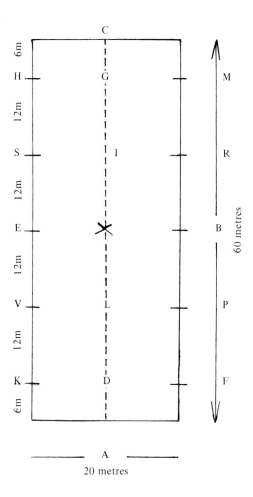

20 metres

This arena is used for all competitions of medium level and over. It is the same width as the novice arena but much longer.

THE NOVICE ARENA

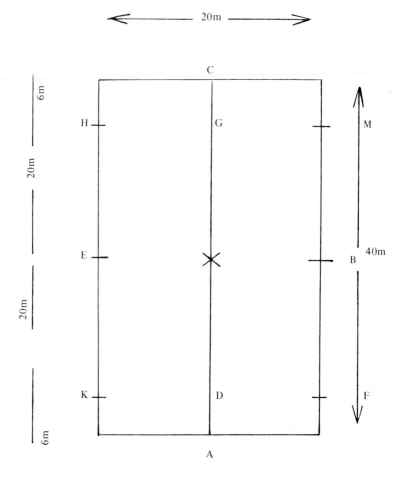

This arena is used for all tests up to
and including elementary level. As you
can see from the diagram it measures
20 metres by 40 metres.

Extended trot, performed by a leading Austrian rider Elisabeth Theurer, on Mon Chéri. The horse uses long strides, but does not move fast.

71

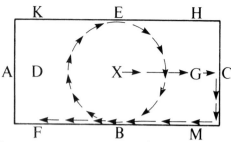

C Track right
B Circle right 20 metres diameter
(sitting) and on returning to
B Working trot (rising)

Explanation

As you will see from the diagram, the competitor on reaching the
C marker turns to the right following the track of the arena. Before
reaching the B marker the rider prepares the horse for a circle by
establishing position right, with the flexion to the right. At the B
marker the rider ceases rising and proceeds on to a circle of 20
metres at the sitting trot. The circle must be round and should
just touch the track at B, E, and just short of D and G. The
competitor, on returning to the B marker, should resume working
trot rising, by going large around the track of the arena.

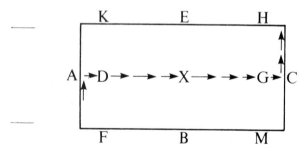

A Down centre line
C Track left

Explanation

At the corner after F, rebalance the horse, keeping the position to
the right. Three yards before the A marker start to turn right. In
this way the competitor will find that the turn is accurate. It is
natural for a horse to lose impulsion on his turn, so the rider must
anticipate by using a firm but active leg aid. Look straight ahead
and it is easy to ride straight. On reaching G, position the horse to
the left, ride forward to C in position left, and then turn left at C.

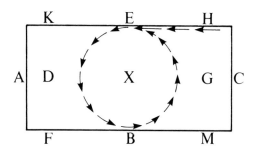

Circle left 20 metres diameter (sitting)

Explanation

The circle should touch the track at E and B just short of D and G. On reaching E marker, cease rising trot, position horse left and commence a large circle to the left maintaining the same rhythm to the trot throughout the circle.

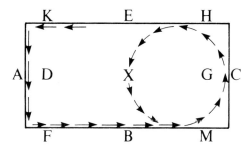

K Working canter left
C Circle left 20 metres diameter

Explanation

At the K marker, ask the horse to canter left, by positioning him left. With inside leg on the girth and outside leg behind the girth, using a positive aid to canter left. The competitor must maintain canter left around the arena until the C marker. On reaching C commence a large circle of 20 metres. The circle must be round and should just touch the track at C, H and M whilst passing through X.

Former World Champion Swiss rider Christine Stukelberger on Granat.

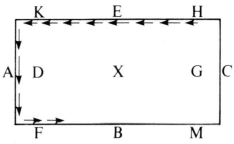

H Working trot
F Medium walk

Explanation

At the corner before H marker prepare to trot, and at H make the transition smoothly to working trot. It is understood that where sitting trot is not specified, then the competitor resumes rising trot. The rider maintains rising trot all the way round the arena passing E, K, A, and on reaching F, the competitor walks. The judges will be looking for a smooth transition, the horse calm and relaxed moving energetically forward between the rider's hand and leg, showing no loss of impulsion or rhythm.

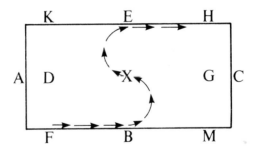

BX Half-circle left 10 metres diameter
XE Half-circle right 10 metres diameter

Explanation

This movement appears at preliminary level and is often badly ridden through lack of planning on the part of the rider. The half-circles must be round with the rhythm of the walk well marked. The half-circle must begin at B, finish at X. On reaching X marker, change the bend of the horse, position him right and ride forward, making a half-circle to E.

Flying change at the canter, performed by Jennie Loriston-Clarke and Dutch Courage.

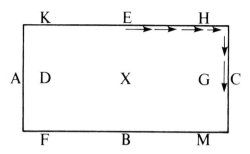

E   Working trot to H
C, M Working canter right

Explanation

This movement is reasonably easy to follow, although care must be taken in the preparation for each movement, ensuring that there is no loss of impulsion, and that the horse moves forward to each transition smoothly, fluently, and accurately. Care must be taken to maintain the bend and outline of the horse thus ensuring that the correct leading leg is achieved.

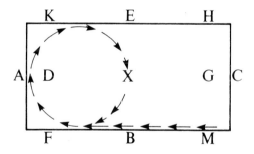

M. B. F.   Working canter
A   Circle right 20 metres

Explanation

In this test the horse is cantering around the arena leading with the off-fore leg. On reaching the A marker the rider commences a large circle of 20 metres. The circle must be round and not a square. The horse should just touch the side of the arena at A and pass through X. The judge will be noticing the balance, rhythm and outline of the horse whilst it maintains a true canter.

Mrs Sievewright, a leading British dressage rider, relaxed after schooling her horse before an advanced competition. The whip is carried for schooling purposes only

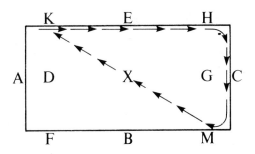

K. E. H. C.   Working trot
M. X. K.   Medium trot

Explanation

Here the horse is trotting around the arena with the competitor
at the rising trot. The stride of the horse should be energetic and
well balanced, the horse accepting the bit and showing good hock
action. On reaching the M marker, the rider prepares to lengthen
the stride of the horse, thus showing the medium trot across the
diagonal.

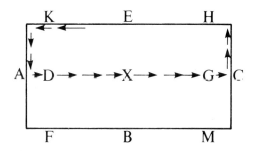

K   Working trot
A   Down centre line
G   Halt salute

Explanation

Here the rider must rebalance the horse and establish position
left, prepare to make a turn at A and ride the horse forward and
straight down the centre line to G, and halt. At G the rider salutes
the judge, not forgetting to smile. After the salute, the horse walks
forward to the C marker, turns left at C and by walking the whole
way around the arena leaves the arena at the A marker.

Helen Gurney (USA) and Keen riding a corner, with the horse bending nicely and full of impulsion.

16 Bits

Under the British Horse Society rules at Preliminary and Novice dressage level an ordinary snaffle only may be worn. *'An ordinary snaffle is a plain snaffle with a straight bar or joint in the centre. If there are two joints, the middle link must be rounded and smooth.'* (Quoted from B.H.S. Rules for Dressage, rule 40.) At Elementary level an ordinary snaffle or a simple double-bridle may be used. In Medium and Advanced competitions a simple double bridle is used.

The snaffle bit is the most commonly used bit on all our horses today. For the purposes of riding competitively, however, the snaffle must have a straight bar, a joint in the middle or, if there are two joints, the middle link must be rounded and smooth. To my certain knowledge there are at least sixty different variations of snaffle bit, and it is thus important to check that the bit one is currently using is in accordance with rule 40 of the B.H.S. Official Rules. Failure to comply with these rules would, of course, incur elimination. It is the competitor's responsibility to know and understand the rules to avoid disappointment and elimination! Below I have listed the bits that are permitted in B.H.S. competitions. At Preliminary, Novice and Elementary level only:-

1. A straight bar snaffle.
2. A snaffle with the mouthpiece made of rubber or nylon.
3. A Fulmer or Australian loose ringed snaffle.
4. A plain cheek snaffle.
5. An egg-butt snaffle.
6. A racing snaffle.
7. A wire ringed ordinary jointed snaffle.
8. An ordinary snaffle with a double-jointed mouthpiece.

Some Examples of Bits used in Preliminary and Novice Tests

A straight bar snaffle

A rubber snaffle

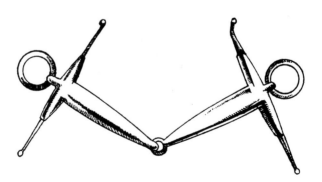

An Australian loose ringed snaffle or Fulmer snaffle

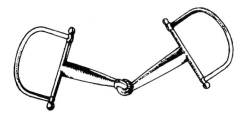

A racing snaffle

A wire ringed jointed snaffle

A snaffle with a double-jointed mouthpiece

83

17 More about the paces of the horse

The walk

There are four types of walk: the medium walk, collected walk, extended walk, and the free walk. Some may wonder how to distinguish one type of walk from another. I believe that they are best recognised by the length of their respective strides, as I will show.

- - - - - - - - -   The collected walk
- - - - - - - - - - - -   The medium walk
- - - - - - - - - - - -   The free walk
- - - - - - - - - - - - - - - - -   The extended walk

From the diagram you will notice that although there are four names given to walk there are only three positive variations to the length of stride.

The walk is a pace of four-time, by which I mean that there are four steps to make one stride at the pace of walk, each step moving separately in succession.

The trained horse that is well balanced and collected will commence from halt with a hind leg first, therefore the sequence is as follows:

1. Near hind
2. Near fore
3. Off hind
4. Off fore

The young horse that is less balanced and perhaps a little on the forehand will commence from halt with a foreleg first, the sequence as follows:

1. Near fore
2. Off hind
3. Off fore
4. Near hind

The Trot

There are four types of trot: the collected trot, working trot, medium trot, and the extended trot. The trots may also be distinguished, by their respective degrees of balance, collection, impulsion, training, and the length of stride.

The collected trot. Only achieved in the well-trained horse who has plenty of impulsion, the trot becoming short, bouncy and elevated.

The working trot. Pace that the young horse uses most before he has the balance to achieve the collected or medium trot. The working trot is used at novice and preliminary level and will

The *passage*, performed by Soviet rider Irina Karacheva riding Said.

appear on the test sheets to be performed at the sitting or rising trot. It is important, therefore, to read the test sheet carefully and notice which is required.

The medium trot. It will be noticed here that the trot stride is longer, the horse therefore covering the ground with good impulsion and balance. The medium trot is used only when the horse's training is such that he has developed an advanced outline and way of going.

The extended trot. At this pace the horse covers the ground with the longest possible stride, the rider will execute the movement at the sitting or the rising trot as shown in the test.

The trot is a pace of two-time, the horse springing alternately from one pair of diagonals to the other.

The right diagonal being the off-fore and the near-hind, the left diagonal the near-fore and the off-hind.

The Canter

There are four types of canter: the collected canter, working canter, medium canter and the extended canter. Canter, as with the other paces, can easily be distinguished by its length of stride, rhythm, impulsion, and regular three-time beat.

The canter is a pace of three-time, by which is meant that there are three definite steps to make one stride at the pace of canter. The sequence of legs is as follows:-

With the near fore-leg leading —

1. Off-hind
2. Right diagonal
3. Near-fore

The collected canter. Similar to the collected trot and can only be achieved by the educated horse. Notice that the length of stride is short.

The working canter. At this pace the horse should be well-balanced and moving freely forward, calmly with a round outline. The working canter is mainly used with the novice horse.

The medium canter. Used with the well-trained horse, the horse covering the ground with a slightly longer stride, maintaining good balance and energy.

The extended canter. This can only successfully be used with the fully trained horse who has sufficient balance and suppleness to cover the ground with the longest possible stride, maintaining the impulsion and rhythm and, of course, on the bit.

Copenhagen 1974 World Championships. Miss Sarah Whitmore riding Junker
— the canter pirouette.

18 Quiz questions for the dressage student

In the next few pages I have posed various questions which, after reading *Dressage Explained*, you may find amusing to answer and a test of your knowledge. For the more serious-minded student wishing to achieve professional qualifications by taking the examinations laid down by the British Horse Society, many of the questions are typical of the type that could be asked at that level.

Q1 Give the sequence of legs at the counter-canter.
A *Inside leg, outside hind and inside fore together with the outside fore taking the last step.*

Q2 What are the aids?
A *The aids are the signals by which the rider conveys his wishes to the horse. They form a common language between horse and rider.*

Q3 What are the main uses of the rider's hands and legs?
A *The inside hand asks for the bend, outside hand controls the pace, inside leg creates energy, outside leg controls the hindquarters.*

Q4 List the points to note when looking at a horse you are thinking of buying.
A *Good length of back (not too short or long)*
A nice depth of girth
Good solid quarters with a gentle slope
A neck well set on to a good pair of gently sloping shoulders
A good width through, leaving plenty of room for the heart and lungs
A good sized head, well set on to the neck, in comparison with the rest of the body
Not too thick through the throat
A good big, kind eye
Cannon bones not too long, flat knees, and pasterns not too short or upright. The hocks well let down and the feet all of the same size and shape (no odd feet)
Tail well set on (not too low or high)
Good open feet with a healthy frog
The horse sound both in wind and limb, with no vices, e.g. kicking, crib-biting, wind sicking, rearing
The horse in good condition throughout, to be a good looker, kind in temperament, and sensible. Most definitely traffic-proof and if possible, a good doer throughout the summer and winter.

Q5 Give notes on circling and explain why circling is a good practise with a young horse.

A *To circle to the right – right leg by the girth, left leg slightly behind the girth, leading with the right rein, left rein lightly supporting. The legs should be on the horse's sides to ensure that the hind feet follow in the tracks of his forefeet. Circling is a good thing, especially with a young horse, as it makes it more supple and obedient and encourages the young horse to use itself.*

Q6 What is free forward movement?

A *Free forward movement is when the horse is willing to go forward at all paces, at all times, at his rider's command.*

Q7 Of the following actions of a horse at the canter, which is said to be true and which disunited?
   a – off-fore followed by off-hind
   b – off-fore followed by near-hind
   c – near-fore followed by near-hind

A a – *Disunited*
   b – *True*
   c – *Disunited*

Q8 Explain the following:
   a – A balanced horse
   b – Collection
   c – True canter
   d – The aids

A *A balanced horse – A horse is said to be balanced when his own weight and that of his rider are placed in such a proportion that he can use himself with maximum ease and efficiency at all paces. His head and neck are the chief factors in weight distribution and it is by their position, either raised or lowered, that the horse carries his centre of gravity backwards or forwards as the paces are collected or extended.*

Collection – A horse is said to be collected when his head is raised, bent at the poll, jaws relaxed, hocks well under him and ready to use himself at the rider's least indication.

True canter is when a horse is cantering with the leading foreleg and the leading hind-leg on the same side.

*The aids are the common language between all horses and riders and they are the signals by which we convey our wishes to the horse. They are divided into two **groups, natural** and artificial.*

Q9 Explain the difference between rhythm and cadence.

A *Rhythm is when the horse as a whole is moving forward with good, even style – the horse moves rhythmically and smoothly.*
Cadence is the rhythm of stride or gait, the beat or timing of stride.
Rhythm is the way the horse moves and Cadence is the rhythm of stride.

Q10 Give a short account of collection and how it is obtained.

A *First of all, one must obtain free forward movement with balance, collection being one extreme of balance, extension being the other. A horse is collected when his head and neck are raised, head bent at the poll with his jaw relaxed, hocks well under him – the horse is likened to a coiled spring, which is ready to spring into action at the slightest command. Having got the horse going and accepting the snaffle bit, to obtain collection one would use change of pace, circling and so on. Walk, halt, trot is one of the best – in fact, the best way to get the horse balanced with his weight in the right place and the bridle so that he will relax his jaw and become collected. Suppleness of the spine and obedience are also all-important in this.*

Q11 How would you proceed with a young horse who was sent to you for schooling, his chief trouble being that he was over-bent?

A *Put him in a snaffle. Remove all gadgets and school him on the flat, asking for more impulsion, sending him on forward and asking for very little – practically no flexion. If he over-bends, send him on forward again on a fairly long rein. Lunging to establish free forward movement again, trying to get some extension, would help.*

Q12 Give the odd one out of walk, trot, canter and gallop.

A *Walk, which has no period of suspension.*

Q13 Name four kinds of trot.

A *Collected, working, medium and extended.*

Q14 Give the timing and sequence of gallop.

A *Four-time. Outside hind, inside hind, outside fore, inside fore.*

Q15 Name the dressage markers in order around an arena, starting at A.
A,K,E,H,C,M,B,F.

Q16 What is tracking up?

A *The movement of the hindfeet falling in the tracks left by the front feet, thereby denoting activity.*

Q17 What is a movement on two tracks?

A *It is a lateral movement in which the front legs travel on a separate track from the hind legs.*

Q18 Give the timing and sequence of rein-back.

A *Rein-back is a pace of two-time, the legs move in diagonal pairs as, for example, near-hind and off-fore together, off-hind and near-fore together.*

Q19 Define step, stride, pace.

A *Step – movement of one leg.*
Stride – completed movement of all four feet.
Pace – gait, that is walk, trot, or canter.

Q20 What do you understand by the term tempo?

A *Tempo is the number of metres to a minute. It is speed.*

Q21 What is rhythm in regard to the horse's pace?

A *Rhythm is regularity of pace. So, if a horse goes unlevel behind, or unlevel round a corner, one can say 'He lost his rhythm at such-and-such corner'.*

Q22 Describe a good halt.

A *The horse should stand motionless with his weight evenly distributed over all four legs, being straight through his spine attentive and alert, the head a little in front of the vertical with the neck raised and the horse flexed from the poll.*

Q23 Give a definition of walk.

A *The walk is a pace of four-time in which the legs move separately in a marching pace, one after another in a sequence of near-fore, off-hind, off-fore, and lastly the near-hind.*

Q24 How should the rider sit at the pace of walk?

A *The rider must sit still with a light rein contact allowing the horse to walk with energetic strides.*

Q25 What do you understand by the term transition?

A *A transition is a change from one pace to another. With the novice horse each of the transitions should be progressive, moving from halt, walk, trot through to canter, or from canter progressively through to walk and halt. All transitions should be carried through gently but distinctly and with plenty of impulsion.*

Q26 What do you understand by free forward movement?

A *A horse is said to be going freely forward on all reins and in all paces, with his energy coming from behind, seeking the rider's hand. Without this forward movement one cannot achieve any of the movements discussed in 'Dressage Explained'.*

Q27 Describe the action of the rider's hands in relation to the dressage horse.

A *The hands, through the reins and the bit in the horse's mouth, control and receive the energy and impulsion produced by the legs. It is also the purpose of the hands to direct and control the head, neck and shoulders of the horse.*

Q28 What do you understand by the travers movement?

A *In travers the horse is bent in his longitudinal form; the outside legs step in front of the inside legs. The horse should be moving forward with impulsion, looking in the direction he is going. Travers is sometimes known as quarters-in as what happens, in effect, is that the rider holds the forehand on the track with both reins, the outside rein having a slightly firmer contact than the inside. The outside leg is supporting the hand and asking the quarters to move to the inside, whilst the inside leg in the normal position at the girth allows the horse to go forward and ensures the correct position of the head and neck, keeping the lateral bend in the horse's body.*

Q29 Describe the renvers movement.

A *This is another exercise to improve the obedience of the horse and make him more supple throughout his joints. In renvers, the quarters stay on the track with the tail to the wall, the horse maintaining the bend of the direction of his travel.*

Q30 What is a demi-pirouette? Describe the movement and how it should be ridden.

A *The demi-pirouette is a turn of 180 degrees normally ridden in the school with the rider asking the horse to bring his forehand round to describe a small circle around the hind-quarters. In effect, therefore, it is a half-turn, on the haunches, the forehand begins the half-turn describing a semi-circle round the haunches, without hesitation, at the moment the inside hindleg stops moving forward. The horse should commence forward movement again, smoothly, without hesitation when the half-turn is completed. To ride a demi-pirouette the aids are as follows: the outside leg is behind the girth, the inside leg on the girth, the inside hand is a direct opening rein asking the horse to take that rein, the outside rein controls the amount of the turn and regulates the speed. Before a good pirouette can be achieved the horse must first be working in the collected paces well and maintaining good forward impulsion.*

Q31　What do you understand by the term contact?

A　　*This is the rein that is held taut from the rider's hand to the bit. The rein is stretched, the lightness and firmness of the contact will vary with each rider and horse.*

Q32　Describe the meaning of tension as related to the handling of the dressage horse.

A　　*Tension is the lightness of contact coupled with firmness and support taken by the horse on the reins.*

Q33　It is often said that a horse is 'above the bit' or 'behind the bit'. Can you explain these two faults?

A　　*Above the bit is when the horse carries his head too high with the bit operating on the corners of the lips instead of the bars of the mouth.*
　　　Behind the bit is when the horse is bringing the angle of his face behind the perpendicular and consequently dropping the bit.

Olympics – Montreal 1976. Miss Sarah Whitmore riding Junker. Warming up before the test.

19 Riders' faults and their corrections

In the first few pages of this book I stressed the importance of practice, training and technique for the dressage rider to develop a correct seat and thus ride by balance and feel, using only the most subtle aids. In order to improve progressively on correct lines it is necessary to have personal advice from a good instructor who is qualified and interested in dressage. I hope that *Dressage Explained* will enable my readers to achieve more in their lessons and will assist in an understanding of the necessary theory explanations that are given by instructors.

I have listed below some of the faults that may occur and when corrected will put the rider on the correct path to success and fun with horses. I hope that it will be remembered that riding is a leisure sport and no matter how seriously taken, it must be fun and a pleasure for both rider and horse.

Fault — Sitting on the back of saddle with stirrups too short.
Remedy — Exercise without stirrups, lengthen leathers gradually.

Fault — Behind the movement with the lower leg too far forward and moving.
Remedy — Stand up in the stirrups at all paces thus finding balance.

Fault — Sitting on the fork, with stirrups too long and leaning forward.
Remedy — Shorten stirrups gradually, swing the arms and look at them.

Fault — Sitting crooked, by collapsing hip or shoulder (mostly right).
Remedy — Trot (rising) with one hand on the back of saddle. Ride with reins in right hand when collapsed on right.

Fault — Hands unsteady with stiff elbows or wrists.
Remedy — Hold a stick like a tray under thumbs. Riding with reins in alternate hands.

Fault — Gripping with lower leg and toes turned out.
Remedy — Try not to grip, rising trot without stirrups, swing lower leg.

Fault — Looking down with stiff shoulders.
Remedy — Ride with other people and watch them, speak when riding. Relax by riding at random in a school with other people.

Conversion tables

WEIGHT kilogrammes	kg or pounds	pounds
0·45	1	2·21
0·91	2	4·41
1·36	3	6·61
1·81	4	8·82
2·27	5	11·02
2·72	6	13·23
3·18	7	15·43
3·63	8	17·64
4·08	9	19·84
4·54	10	22·05
9·07	20	44·09
13·61	30	66·14
18·14	40	88·19
22·68	50	110·2
27·22	60	132·3
31·75	70	154·3
36·29	80	176·4
40·82	90	198·4
45·36	100	220·5

VOLUME litres	litres or gallons	gallons
4·55	1	0·22
9·09	2	0·44
13·64	3	0·66
18·18	4	0·88
22·73	5	1·10
27·28	6	1·32
31·82	7	1·54
36·37	8	1·76
40·91	9	1·98
45·46	10	2·20
90·92	20	4·40
136·4	30	6·60
181·8	40	8·80
227·3	50	11·00
272·8	60	13·20
318·2	70	15·40
363·7	80	17·60
409·1	90	19·80
454·6	100	22·00

Temperature Conversion

Celsius	-18°	-10	0	10	20	30	40°
Fahrenheit	0°	10	20	32 40	50 60	70 80	90 100 110°

$$C = \frac{5}{9}(F - 32) \qquad F = \frac{9}{5}C + 32$$

LENGTH centimetres	cm or inches	inches
2·54	1	0·39
5·08	2	0·79
7·62	3	1·18
10·16	4	1·58
12·70	5	1·97
15·24	6	2·36
17·78	7	2·76
20·32	8	3·15
22·86	9	3·54
25·40	10	3·94
50·80	20	7·87
76·20	30	11·81
101·6	40	15·75
127·0	50	19·69
152·4	60	23·62
177·8	70	27·56
203·2	80	31·50
228·6	90	35·43
254·0	100	39·37

kilometres	km or miles	miles
1·61	1	0·62
3·22	2	1·24
4·83	3	1·86
6·44	4	2·49
8·05	5	3·11
9·66	6	3·73
11·27	7	4·35
12·88	8	4·97
14·48	9	5·59
16·09	10	6·21
32·19	20	12·43
48·28	30	18·64
64·37	40	24·86
80·47	50	31·07
96·56	60	37·28
112·7	70	43·50
128·7	80	49·71
144·8	90	55·92
160·9	100	62·14